EXODUS

THEOLOGY OF WORK   PROJECT

EXODUS

THE BIBLE AND YOUR WORK
Study Series

HENDRICKSON
PUBLISHERS

Theology of Work
The Bible and Your Work Study Series: Exodus

© 2015 by Hendrickson Publishers Marketing, LLC
P.O. Box 3473
Peabody, Massachusetts 01961-3473

ISBN 978-1-61970-683-5

Adapted from the *Theology of Work Bible Commentary*, copyright © 2014 by the Theology of Work Project, Inc. All rights reserved.

William Messenger, Executive Editor, Theology of Work Project
Sean McDonough, Biblical Editor, Theology of Work Project
Patricia Anders, Editorial Director, Hendrickson Publishers

Contributors:
Christopher Gilbert, "Exodus" Bible Study
Bob Stallman, "Exodus and Work" in the *Theology of Work Bible Commentary*

The Theology of Work Project is an independent, international organization dedicated to researching, writing, and distributing materials with a biblical perspective on work. The Project's primary mission is to produce resources covering every book of the Bible plus major topics in today's workplaces. Wherever possible, the Project collaborates with other faith-and-work organizations, churches, universities and seminaries to help equip people for meaningful, productive work of every kind.

Printed in the United States of America

First Printing—September 2015

Contents

The Theology of Work

Work is not only a human calling, but also a divine one. "In the beginning God created the heavens and the earth." God worked to create us and created us to work. "The LORD God took the man and put him in the garden of Eden to till it and keep it" (Gen. 2:15). God also created work to be good, even if it's hard to see in a fallen world. To this day, God calls us to work to support ourselves and to serve others (Eph. 4:28).

Work can accomplish many of God's purposes for our lives—the basic necessities of food and shelter, as well as a sense of fulfillment and joy. Our work can create ways to help people thrive; it can discover the depths of God's creation; and it can bring us into wonderful relationships with co-workers and those who benefit from our work (customers, clients, patients, and so forth).

Yet many people face drudgery, boredom, or exploitation at work. We have bad bosses, hostile relationships, and unfriendly work environments. Our work seems useless, unappreciated, faulty, frustrating. We don't get paid enough. We get stuck in dead-end jobs or laid off or fired. We fail. Our skills become obsolete. It's a struggle just to make ends meet. But how can this be if God created work to be good—and what can we do about it? God's answers for these questions must be somewhere in the Bible, but where?

The Theology of Work Project's mission has been to study what the Bible says about work and to develop resources to apply the Christian faith to our work. It turns out that every book of the Bible gives practical, relevant guidance that can help us do our jobs better, improve our relationships at work, support ourselves, serve others more effectively, and find meaning and value in our work. The Bible shows us how to live all of life—including work—in Christ. Only in Jesus can our work be transformed to become the blessing it was always meant to be.

To put it another way, if we are not following Christ during the 100,000 hours of our lives that we spend at work, are we really following Christ? Our lives are more than just one day a week at church. The fact is that God cares about our life *every day of the week*. But how do we become equipped to follow Jesus at work? In the same ways we become equipped for every aspect of life in Christ—listening to sermons, modeling our lives on others' examples, praying for God's guidance, and most of all by studying the Bible and putting it into practice.

This Theology of Work series contains a variety of books to help you apply the Scriptures and Christian faith to your work. This Bible study is one volume in the series The Bible and Your Work. It is intended for those who want to explore what the Bible says about work and how to apply it to their work in positive, practical ways. Although it can be used for individual study, Bible study is especially effective with a group of people committed to practicing what they read in Scripture. In this way, we gain from one another's perspectives and are encouraged to actually *do* what we read in Scripture. Because of the direct focus on work, The Bible and Your Work studies are especially suited for Bible studies *at* work or *with* other people in similar occupations. The following lessons are designed for thirty-minute lunch breaks, although they can be used in other formats as well.

Christians today recognize God's calling to us in and through our work—for ourselves and for those whom we serve. May God use this book to help you follow Christ in every sphere of life and work.

Will Messenger, Executive Editor
Theology of Work Project

Introduction to Exodus

The story of Exodus opens and closes with ancient Israel at work. In the beginning, the Israelites are Egyptian slaves. By the book's end, they are a free people, who complete the creation of a magnificent portable tabernacle, according to the instruction and design of the God who freed them (Exod. 40:33). How this happens is the issue for us in Exodus.

In this book we will discover that God's character is revealed in his work. And as we are drawn to the person he reveals himself to be, his work shapes our work. So we approach this study of the theology of work by asking who our Creator and Redeemer reveals himself to be in the book of Exodus and how we can follow him so that we become like him.

As God reveals more of his character, we discover how this influences human life as he shapes a people for himself. The experience of the Israelites accords to our experience as Christians today. Unless we are drawn to God by his Spirit and the uniqueness of his redeeming work in Christ, our work will not harmonize with his ongoing work. In fact, our work can be out of sync with his purposes, or worse, oppose his will. In our study we will discover that following God in our work *is* a significant topic in Exodus, even though work is not the primary point of the book.

Although much in Exodus speaks to everyday work, the instructions take place in a world three thousand years past. We understand that some passages, such as "You shall not commit murder" (Exod. 20:13), transcend time and are as relevant now as then. But others, such as "If someone's ox hurts the ox of another, so that it dies, then they shall sell the live ox and divide the price of it" (Exod. 21:35), are a long way removed from most twenty-first-century lives in developed countries. The challenge for us is to make sense of their laws without falling into the traps of either legalistic or dismissive interpretations.

In that regard, it is helpful to remember that Exodus is a narrative. Just as it helped ancient Israel to locate itself in God's story, it helps us to find out today how we fit into the more comprehensive story of redemption. Through this story, God's work frames our identity as his people, as well as directs the work God has called us to do. Because God did not deliver Israel *from* work. He set Israel free *for* work.

Chapter 1

Israel in Egypt

Lesson #1: The Harshness of Israel's Slavery in Egypt (Exodus 1:1–14)

As our story begins, we discover a people who have followed the creation mandate of the Genesis account: they have been fruitful and they have multiplied (Gen. 1:28; 9:1). We are meant to recall this God-given mandate, as well as God's promise to Abraham to bless the world through his chosen descendants (Gen. 17:6; 35:11; 47:27). A previous Egyptian pharaoh had gladly provided Jacob and his family with land to work and develop. But many generations later, another pharaoh is threatened by their numbers, and from fear for the safety of his own race, he imposes an increasingly oppressive slavery on the Israelites. Then he tries to curb their population growth by murdering the males at birth. This mistreatment provides the background and impetus for Israel's deliverance.

 Food for Thought

Fear is a cruel master of those who don't resist it. And its impact on others in our workplaces is often a matter of degree—from mild imposition to fierce oppression. Can you think of a fear you suffered that impacted badly in your workplace? What were the effects? Discuss strategies for avoiding fear-based decisions.

As noted in Genesis 1–11, work in a fallen world is physically
and mentally taxing. Things keep going wrong. Creativity is con-
stantly compromised by the constant need for maintenance and
repair in our work as a result of deliberate sabotage or simple
human error. But this doesn't necessarily make work evil.

What makes the situation in Egypt unbearable is not only the
forced labor. The Egyptian masters worked the Israelites "ruth-
lessly" (*befarekh*, Exod. 1:13–14) and made their lives "bitter"
(*marar*, Exod. 1:14) with "hard" (*qasheh*, in the sense of "cruel,"
Exod. 1:14; 6:9) service. As a result, Israel languished in "misery"
and "suffering" (Exod. 3:7) and a "broken spirit" (Exod. 6:9).
Work, one of the chief purposes and joys of human existence
(Gen. 1:27–31; 2:15), was turned into a misery by the violence
of oppression.

Forced labor was common in the ancient world, and it continues
to exist today. According to the International Labor Organization, 21 million people are in forced labor, of which 11 million
are women and girls and 9 million men and boys. Sex trafficking accounts for 20 percent of the total, while domestic work,
agriculture, construction, manufacturing, and entertainment
account for most of the rest.

An example is shrimp (prawn) fishing in Thailand, as reported
in 2014 in the British newspaper *The Guardian*. Few Thais are
willing to take jobs in the fishing industry due to low pay and
poor working conditions, exploitation, and abuse. So the indus-

try depends on labor brokers to supply 80 percent of its 145,000 workers. The brokers recruit migrant workers, both men and women, from distant regions or countries with promises of jobs in food processing, agriculture, or manufacturing. The workers are then forced to work on fishing boats. The average pay is 75 percent of Thailand's daily minimum wage.

Many of these fishing boats do not return to port for months at a time, meaning that the captain has complete control over the working and living conditions of these workers. Although not all of them are in actual forced labor, 57 percent have experienced one or more conditions of forced labor. The most common conditions include being allowed no contact outside the workplace (94 percent), sexual or physical violence (68 percent), injury (47 percent), lack of food (44 percent), wage reductions (42 percent), and being locked into their rooms when not on duty (23 percent). More than half have no defined working hours, meaning they often work seventeen or more hours a day.

Labor exploitation also occurs in developed countries. As with the Israelites in Egypt, workers with precarious immigration status are especially vulnerable to exploitation. For example, the *Boston Globe* reported in 2012 that the Upper Crust Pizza chain recruited undocumented workers from the village of Marilac, Brazil, housing them in a decrepit company-provided apartment, and deducting rent from their pay. The company underpaid workers for eighty-hour work weeks and was ordered by the United States Department of Labor to pay workers $350,000 in back pay in 2009. In response, Upper Crust Pizza paid the workers, but then deducted the amount from future paychecks until caught again in 2012 and ordered to pay workers $850,000 in back pay and damages. The company escaped making payments by declaring bankruptcy.

Similarly, in 2015 the *New York Times* reported widespread worker exploitation in nail salons, including charging workers a fee to become employees, paying workers a fraction of minimum wage, not paying overtime, requiring sixty-plus-hour work weeks, including some days with no pay, skimming tips, charging workers for drinking water, physical abuse, illegally deducting pay for infractions such as spilling nail polish, prohibiting workers from talking, and paying different wages based on workers' ethnicities.

 Food for Thought

The struggle against slavery and forced labor stretches back thousands of years. God's intervention to liberate his people from slavery is the foundational narrative of the nation of Israel. Regrettably, Christians have nonetheless sometimes participated in or benefitted from slavery. Is it possible that you are benefitting from others' forced labor? Does your employer outsource labor to places where working conditions are impossible to verify? Are there harsh practices and inequalities needing reform where you work?

_____

_____

_____

_____

_____

_____

_____

Prayer

Pause for a few moments of silence to reflect on this lesson. Then offer a prayer, either spontaneous or by using the following:

Lord,

You delivered Israel with a "mighty hand and an out-stretched arm" and sent your Son to bring us freedom from every form of bondage. Help us become aware of the work of people who are not free and to overcome the apathy or confusion that would keep us from acting on their behalf.

Amen.

Lesson #2: Midwives and a Mother Recognize Evil and Defy It (Exodus 1:15–2:10)

Childbirth and mothering are often overlooked as labor for the common good. And until recently, not many stories were told of the heroism of mothers and those who assist them. One cultural corrective to that blind spot is the story of a nursing mission of Anglican nuns in the 1950s as portrayed in the BBC dramatic series, *Call the Midwife.* In this story, young midwives help the nuns deliver children in the impoverished East End of London—children who might otherwise die in childbirth. When Exodus (a book filled with courageous deeds) begins, the first act of courage is that of a mother, her family, and Egyptian midwives in saving her child.

In an attempt at genocide, Pharaoh orders that every male Hebrew child be killed at birth. But the women responsible for bringing life into the world respond to their sense of call from a higher authority. They "fear God" and refuse to cooperate, even lying to the king to protect the children. And as "God dealt well with the midwives," their story underscores the incomparable importance to God of ensuring life and nurture for children.

 Food for Thought

Following God may require decisions that can put us at risk. In your workplace, have you ever received a command to do something against your conscience or that contradicted your biblically informed values? If so, how did you respond?

_____

_____

_____

_____

_____

_____

_____

Moses' mother Jochebed (Exod. 6:20) faces an apparently impossible choice and forges a creative solution. We can hardly imagine her relief at secretly and successfully bearing a male child, followed by her pain at having to place him into the river, but in a way that would actually save his life. As he does for the midwives, God shows kindness to Jochebed. She recovers her son and nurses him until he is old enough to be adopted as the son of Pharaoh's daughter. From a narrative point of view, Moses' life is the main issue of the unfolding story. But the Bible later commends both Jochebed and Moses' father for how they put their faith into action (Heb. 11:23).

 *Food for Thought*

What are some instances in your experience, or the experience of others, when a work situation was so appalling and dangerous that it was necessary to deceive the perpetrators of the injustice?

_____

_____

_____

_____

_____

Prayer

Pause for a few moments of silence to reflect on this lesson. Then offer a prayer, either spontaneous or by using the following:

> *Lord,*
>
> *When situations come at us that seem so contrary to your character and values, please help us as we wrestle with finding an appropriate response. We commit ourselves to you to be those who don't give up when everything seems to be getting darker. Help us to keep looking forward in the certainty that you see and know what we suffer.*
>
> *Amen.*

Lesson #3: God's Call to Moses (Exodus 2:11–3:22)

Despite his Hebrew identity, Moses is raised in Egypt's royal family as the grandson of Pharaoh. Observing the brutal treatment of his own people, his anger explodes on an Egyptian taskmaster, whom he kills in the act of beating a Hebrew slave. When

Pharaoh learns of the crime, Moses flees for safety and becomes a shepherd in Midian, a region several hundred miles east of Egypt on the other side of the Sinai Peninsula.

After he has been there for some decades, two important events occur. The king in Egypt dies, and the Lord hears the cry of his oppressed people and remembers his covenant with Abraham, Isaac, and Jacob (Exod. 2:23–25). This did not mean that God had forgotten about his people. It signaled that now the time was right to act on their behalf. To that purpose he calls Moses.

 Food for Thought

Sometimes we intuit God's intention for us but get the timing and even the big picture of it wrong. What can we learn from this section of the story about God's call and his sense of time, and ours?

_____

_____

_____

_____

_____

When God calls him, Moses is busy herding sheep. We see this happening throughout Scripture: people were busy working when God called them to take action. Likewise, this has implications for us in the context of our own work lives. Here is an outline of how the Lord called Moses:

1. God attracts Moses' attention through a strange phenomenon—a bush that burns without being consumed. As Moses

draws near, he hears his name called. He replies, "Here I am," meaning that he is available and listening.

2. The Lord reveals himself as the God of Moses' revered forebears—Abraham, Isaac, and Jacob—who is now about to rescue his people from Egypt and bring them into the land he had promised to Abraham (Exod. 3:6–9).

3. God commissions Moses to go to Pharaoh to accomplish this exodus from Egypt (Exod. 3:10).

4. Because he doubts himself, Moses objects (Exod. 3:11), asking, "Who am I that I should go to Pharaoh, and bring the Israelites out of Egypt?"

5. God reassures Moses with a promise of God's own presence (Exod. 3:12a).

6. God speaks of a confirming sign (Exod. 3:12b).

 Food for Thought

When you consider the pattern of your work life, do you sense any of the above elements in your own life? In what ways might you be called to be a blessing through what you do? What excuses do you make for holding back?

_____

_____

_____

_____

_____

_____

We see these same elements in a number of other call narratives in Scripture—the stories of Gideon, Isaiah, Jeremiah, Ezekiel, and some of Jesus' disciples. Although many of these call narratives follow a different pattern, it still suggests that God's call will come to our attention through circumstances and events over a period of time.

Most of the callings in Scripture are not calls to priestly, or what we might now call "pastoral," occupations. Gideon was called to serve as a military leader, Isaiah, Jeremiah, and Ezekiel as social critics, and Jesus as a king (although not in the sense of governing one nation among many). In many churches today, the term "call" is limited to religious occupations, but this is not so in Scripture, and certainly not in Exodus. Moses was not a priest or religious leader (those were Aaron's and Miriam's roles), but a statesman, judge, and governor. (For more on calling to nonreligious work, see "Vocation Overview" at www.theologyofwork.org.)

 Food for Thought

What unites all kinds of callings is God's purpose that we serve people through our work. But it's not always easy to discern what our calls are. Who among your co-workers seems to operate with a clear sense of call? Write down a few questions you could ask this person about how they came to recognize the calling.

_____

_____

_____

_____

_____

_____

Prayer

Pause for a few moments of silence to reflect on this lesson. Then offer a prayer, either spontaneous or by using the following:

Lord,

We live in a world of many loud voices. Please help us in the midst of the noise to notice your voice, and what you may be doing to attract our notice. Help us to believe we have been made for a purpose beyond the smallness of our imaginations. Speak, Lord, for I am listening.

Amen.

Chapter 2

God's Work of Redemption for Israel

Lesson #1: Redemption Is Entirely God's Work (Exodus 5:1–6:9)

In the book of Exodus, God is the essential worker. The nature and intent of that divine work sets the agenda for Moses' work and, through him, the work of God's people. God's initial call to Moses explains this so clearly that Moses is compelled to speak in the name of the Lord to Pharaoh saying, "Let my people go" (Exod. 5:1).

Pharaoh's rebuttal is not merely verbal; he oppresses the Israelites even more harshly so that the Israelites themselves turn against Moses (Exod. 5:20–21). In Moses' anguish over this response, he questions what God is asking of him. God clarifies it for him, and for us, in the part of the story found in Exodus 6:2–8.

 Food for Thought

Armed with the sense of God's mission for him, what do you think Moses imagined as an outcome of his visit to Pharaoh? Have you ever had a similar experience where you had to make a serious request to a person of power? If you were denied your request (like Moses with Pharaoh multiple times), how did you respond? What happened next?

Responding to God leads Moses into failure after failure and makes him deeply unpopular with the people he came to serve. The ancient prophets experienced similar suffering and persecution at the hands of Israel's kings and people. Suffering as a result of responding to God's call is a common biblical theme that reaches its climax in the life of Jesus. This explains why Jesus counsels us to pray for God's kingdom to come and for his will to be done on earth as it is in heaven (Matt. 6:10). As long as God's will is *not* being done here, those who follow God's calling will inevitably suffer. "Thy will be done on earth, as it is in heaven" is a prayer to make the suffering stop. As the Apostle Paul would later say to one of the early churches, the kingdom of God comes through much tribulation (Acts 14:21–22).

The fulfillment of this redemption of humanity—God's kingdom come—*is* God's business. To accomplish it, he will commission people to an extraordinary diversity of occupations, not merely those who do "religious" work. God calls people to every task that helps make the world more as God has always intended it to be. As we gain a clearer understanding of God's work, its scope and continuity through the ages, we are equipped to appreciate not only the nature of our own work but the manner in which God intends for us to do it.

 *Food for Thought*

How does Exodus 6:2–8 help you appreciate the Lord's Prayer in Matthew 6:10–13? In what ways might this assist you to be confident in the purpose of your own work? If you don't feel confident, ask yourself why and what you could do about it.

_____

_____

_____

_____

_____

_____

_____

Lesson #2: Redemption in Four Movements (Exodus 7:1–15:21)

In Exodus, God's work of redemption unfolds in four discernible movements. We see this work throughout the Old Testament, and it foreshadows the pinnacle of God's redemptive work in Jesus Christ. In this lesson we will outline these four movements and reflect briefly on their implications for our work.

First is the work of deliverance. "I will free you from the burdens of the Egyptians and deliver you from slavery to them. I will redeem you with an outstretched arm and with mighty acts of judgment" (Exod. 6:6). This work of deliverance acknowledges the sad, historical normality of human oppression. But the God of Israel shows that he does care and in one of the most remarkable stories ever recorded, he delivers his people from a life of slavery.

 *Food for Thought*

Are there are any instances of oppression in your workplace? Do you know if your organization participates in unethical practices or benefits from oppressive conditions elsewhere? If so, what can you do about it?

_____

_____

_____

_____

_____

_____

_____

Second, the Lord enables his people to be a godly community. "I will take you as my people, and I will be your God" (Exod. 6:7a). God intends to create a qualitatively different kind of *community* in which his people live with him and one another in covenantal faithfulness. They are not delivered as lone individuals free to live and work as they please, but as a community called to work for one another's well-being. Israel's identity as God's people entails a lifestyle of obedience to all of God's decrees, commands, and laws (Deut. 26:17–18). In this way, God commissions Israel to become a people who reflect the character of God to the whole world, distinguishing them from all the other nations and their "gods."

Third, the Lord establishes an ongoing relationship between himself and his people. "You shall know that I am the Lord your God, who has freed you from the burdens of the Egyptians" (Exod. 6:7b). When God says "You shall know," he means relationally, that he is working with them in a personal way. Abraham came to know God through his experience of being guided and guarded as a nomad in an already occupied land. And Moses came to know him as the voice of the same promise-keeping God who would fight on behalf of his people as a nation and deliver them from slavery.

Fourth, God provides for his people to experience an abundant life. "I will bring you into the land that I swore to give to Abraham, Isaac, and Jacob; I will give it to you for a possession" (Exod. 6:8). God promises Abraham the land of Canaan, but it is not accurate to simply equate this "land" with our concept of a "region." The "land" includes the rich harvest from the land that God promises, so it is a promise of fruitfulness and provision. The description of it as "flowing with milk and honey" symbolizes it as a place to live with God and his people in peace and harmony, something we understand as the abundant life. So, again we see that God's work of salvation sets to right his entire creation—the environment, people, cultures, economics. In a word, *everything*.

 Food for Thought

How would you define "abundant life"? To what extent does your work contribute to your "abundant life"? What about others with or for whom you work?

_____

_____

_____

_____

_____

Prayer

Pause for a few moments of silence to reflect on this lesson. Then offer a prayer, either spontaneous or by using the following:

> *Lord,*
>
> *In our workplace, help us to be a community that reflects your justice and beauty, grace and truth, fruitfulness and provision for our mutual needs. Thank you for your words of assurance that as we take action according to your character, you promise to be in our midst.*
>
> *Amen.*

Lesson #3: Modern-Day Justice at Work (Exodus 6:10–13)

One industry pioneer who modeled how to bring deliverance to hostile working conditions is Wayne Alderson (1926–2013), who was vice president of Pittron Steel near Pittsburgh in the early 1970s. The company had hostile labor/management relationships, and was facing a strike that could destroy the company. Although management's approach to these negotiations was confrontational, partway into the strike, Alderson began an effort of reconciliation with the union. "They are not our enemy," he said. "They are the people who do our work." He was tough, but fair, and demonstrated his respect for the union workers. He developed an approach he called "Value of the Person," which not only achieved a settlement of the strike, but also transformed the working environment of the company, restoring it to profitability. "Everyone wants to be treated with love, dignity, and respect," Alderson said.

 *Food for Thought*

What elements of the four movements in redemption appear in the pioneering work of Wayne Alderson? What surprises you in this brief outline of his story? What may be applicable to your work situation?

_____

_____

_____

_____

_____

_____

_____

_____

Prayer

Pause for a few moments of silence to reflect on this lesson. Then offer a prayer, either spontaneous or by using the following:

> *Lord,*
>
> *We recognize that our workplaces are always in danger of becoming hostile or oppressive. Please help us respond to any issues in our workplaces that diminish people made in your image. Grant us eyes to see and courage to seek the necessary changes.*
>
> *Amen.*

Chapter 3

Judgment on Egypt and the Flight through the Wilderness to Sinai

Lesson #1: God's Work of Redemption for His People (Exodus 15:22–17:16)

God initiates the first step toward redemption of the Israelites by calling Moses and Aaron to tell Pharaoh "to let the Israelites go out of his land" (Exod. 7:2). He engages Aaron to use his natural skill in public speaking (4:14; 7:1), and he also equips Aaron with power surpassing that of the magicians of Egypt (7:10–12). Eloquence and practical skill are matched with obedient action as a means to precipitate change.

Pharaoh refuses to listen to God's demand through Moses to release Israel from slavery. In turn, Moses announces God's judgment to Pharaoh through an increasingly severe series of ecological disasters (7:17–10:29). These disasters cause many layers of misery.

Most significantly, the disasters God delivers wreck the productivity of Egypt's land and people. Disease causes livestock to die (9:6), crops fail and forests are ruined (9:25), and pests invade multiple ecosystems (8:6, 24; 10:13–15). In our own time, we have witnessed how political and corporate oppression has caused or exacerbated ecological disasters. We would be foolish to think we

can assume Moses' authority and declare God's judgment in any
of these. But we can see that when economics, politics, culture,
and society are in need of redemption, so is the environment.

 Food for Thought

It is more common these days to recognize there are "best practices" to follow in our workplaces (points of action designed for
the safety or well-being of workers and clients). Name a simple
form of best practices in your own field of work. What happens
if these practices are ignored or deliberately subverted for the
unjust or short-term gain of an individual or small group? How
would you respond if you saw that happening?

_____

_____

_____

_____

_____

_____

_____

_____

After each disaster befalls Egypt, Pharaoh relents at first but
then changes his mind. Finally, God brings on the disaster of
slaying all the firstborn among the people and animals of the
Egyptians (12:29–30).

The loss of the firstborn of Egypt dramatizes that slavery exacts
a grievous toll on slave owners. Although they may benefit eco-

nomically, their hearts are inevitably "hardened" as Pharaoh's was, and the final consequences are disastrous, both physically and spiritually (11:10). It is only in the suffering of great personal loss that Pharaoh accepts God's demand to let Israel go free. When the departing Israelites plunder the Egyptians' jewelry, silver, gold, and clothing (12:35–36), this reverses the effects of slavery, which was the legalized plunder of workers' labor. When God liberates the people, he restores their right to the fruits of their labor, for their own enjoyment (Isa. 65:21–22). Work and the conditions under which it is performed are matters of the highest concern to God.

 Food for Thought

Consider the effect of whistleblowing upon corrupt behavior. How alike is it to the task of Moses and Aaron? What is different? Do you know about any corrupt behavior in your workplace? If so, what can you do about it?

_____

_____

_____

_____

_____

_____

_____

Prayer

Pause for a few moments of silence to reflect on this lesson. Then offer a prayer, either spontaneous or by using the following:

> *Lord,*
>
> *Help us to recognize the value of others' work. Draw our attention to any ways we may be unfairly claiming the fruit of other people's labor. Grant that we might address the issues we know about with all wisdom and reliance upon you! So help us be obedient children of light.*
>
> *Amen.*

Lesson #2: The Work of Justice among the People of Israel (Exodus 18:1–23)

After the experience of injustice administered by their Egyptian taskmasters, the escaped Israelites must administer justice for themselves. God's redemption of Israel now includes developing a system of justice according to his original design. Walter Brueggemann suggests that biblical faith includes "the hard, sustained work of nurturing and practicing the daily passion of healing and restoring, and the daily rejection of dishonest gain."

It is while burdened down by taking that huge responsibility on himself that Moses receives a visit from his father-in-law, Jethro. Although an outsider to the tribes of Israel, he offers much-needed counsel to Moses on a better way to deliver justice.

 *Food for Thought*

How is justice administered in your workplace? Who takes responsibility for resolving disputes, nurturing best practices, hiring and firing? How well does the system work?

_____

_____

_____

_____

_____

Before he fled Egypt, when Moses tried to mediate between two Israelites in dispute, they rebuked him, "Who made you a ruler and a judge over us?" (Exod. 2:14). Now the tables are turned. Moses is in such demand as the ruler-judge that a multitude of people in need of his decisions gather around him "from morning until evening" (Exod. 18:14; see also Deut. 1:9–18). He seems to operate at two levels. First, he renders legal decisions for people in dispute. Second, he teaches his people God's statutes and instructions so they can live as the people of God.

Jethro can see that the entire process is unsustainable. Moses is a bottleneck to justice for a huge number of people, and the effort for Moses is all-consuming. Jethro urges him to delegate any duties that could be performed by others, which frees Moses for what he is uniquely qualified to do as God's representative: intercede with God for the people, instruct them, and decide their difficult cases. All of the other cases are then delegated to subordinate judges who will serve in a four-tiered system of judicial administration.

 *Food for Thought*

Do you hold on to tasks that could be better delegated to other people? Is it possible that there others in your work group or community who would be willing and able to take on some of your tasks, if you would let them? If so, who and what?

_____

_____

_____

_____

_____

_____

_____

_____

The wisdom of Jethro's plan is in the qualifications required of the judges. They could not be selected by tribal division of the people or by perceived religious or social ranking, and they had to meet four qualifications (Exod. 18:21).

1. They must be capable. In Hebrew, "able men" (*hayil*) connotes ability, leadership, management, resourcefulness, and due respect.

2. They must "fear God." This is the same term used to describe the midwives; it does not mean people who are especially religious, but people of good moral character.

3. They must be "men of truth," with a publicly honored record of truthful conduct and character.

4. They must be haters of unjust gain. They must know how and why corruption occurs, despise the practice of bribery and all kinds of subversion, and actively guard the judicial process from these infections.

Food for Thought

Consider each of these four qualifications and discuss the implications of each requirement as applied in your own work situation.

_____

_____

_____

_____

_____

_____

Prayer

Pause for a few moments of silence to reflect on this lesson. Then offer a prayer, either spontaneous or by using the following:

Lord,

Make our communities to be places where justice is administered and practiced daily, so that we may discover the freedom of life as you made it to be. Grant that we might include in our work "the hard, sustained work of nurturing and practicing the daily passion of healing and restoring, and the daily rejection of dishonest gain."

Amen.

Lesson #3: The Gift of Delegating Power (Exodus 18:24–27)

Delegation of power to make judgments is essential to the work of justice. Though Moses is uniquely gifted as a prophet, statesman, and judge, he is constrained by his mortal nature to a limited amount of time and energy. It's a foolish person who tries to live beyond the body's need for rest and recuperation.

Competence in delegation is ultimately a gift from God. Moses has to discern the qualities needed, train those who will receive authority, and then develop the means to hold them accountable. Even Moses needs to make himself accountable, which he does with his father-in-law. Jethro is the older and wiser leader, and Moses recognizes that his advice is a gift from God.

 Food for Thought

What experiences have you had as a delegator, or as one who has been delegated power to act? How have you enjoyed the experience? Or if it was a poor experience, why?

_____

_____

_____

_____

_____

_____

_____

Wise, decisive, compassionate leadership is a gift from God that every human community needs. Yet Exodus shows us that it is not so much a matter of a gifted leader assuming authority over people, as it is God's process for a community to develop structures of leadership in which gifted people can succeed.

Delegation is the only way to increase the capacity of an institution or community, as well as the way to develop future leaders. The fact that Moses accepted this counsel so quickly and thoroughly may be evidence that he recognized the urgency of his need. Through this he exercised the humility for which God honors him before Aaron and Miriam. But the story is even more interesting because Moses was open to God's wisdom mediated to him through someone outside the people of Israel.

 Food for Thought

How is this kind of leadership "God's process"? How does this play out in your workplace, even in a non-Christian environment? Do you have "structures of leadership in which gifted people can succeed"?

Moses' humble response to Jethro should encourage us to receive and respect input from others who have more wisdom and experience in our field of work. Being open to the diverse sources of "best practices" is not a mark of disloyalty to Christ. It is not about a lack of confidence in our faith. Rather, we need to see that God, who *made* the world in its diversity, wants us to open ourselves to every good gift, which sometimes may be beyond the limits of our knowledge and experience, yet harmonious with Scripture and instituted by him.

Prayer

Pause for a few moments of silence to reflect on this lesson. Then offer a prayer, either spontaneous or by using the following:

Lord,

Thank you for how Moses held himself accountable in the power he exercised. Grant that we too might be willing to act transparently and trust those you bring to us as helpers with the exercise of our own power. Help us also to be open and willing to receive wisdom and knowledge from all the diverse sources you provide.

Amen.

Chapter 4

Israel at Mount Sinai

At Mount Sinai, Moses receives the Ten Commandments from the Lord. However, the role of the Israelite law for Christians has been a matter of debate since the dawn of the church. To help us navigate the difficulties, we will be attentive to what the text of Exodus actually says. At the same time, we hope to be aware and respectful of the variety of ways that Christians may wish to draw lessons from this part of the Bible.

Lesson #1: The Meaning of Law in Exodus (Exodus 19:1–25)

Theologian Christopher Wright suggests, "The common opinion that the Bible is a moral code book for Christians falls far short, of course, of the full reality of what the Bible is and does." Of course the Scriptures are a grand narrative of God at work in making and saving humanity and the world. But Wright is correct to say, "The Bible's demand is for the appropriate response from human beings. God's mission calls for and includes human response. And our mission certainly includes the ethical dimension of that response." So we begin this lesson by recognizing that Exodus is integral to the entire biblical narrative. It is not a stand-alone book of legal statutes.

 *Food for Thought*

As you read Exodus, what is your first response when you come to the law given at Sinai? What questions does it raise for you?

_____

_____

_____

_____

_____

_____

_____

The English word *law* is a traditional yet inaccurate rendering of the key Hebrew word *Torah*. Because this term is so central to our discussion, we need to appreciate how it actually works in the Bible. "Torah" appears once in Genesis as instructions from God that Abraham followed (Gen. 26:5). Although it can refer to instructions from one human to another (Ps. 78:1), we usually find "Torah" as instructions from God. Throughout the first five books of Scripture (the Pentateuch) and the rest of the Old Testament, it means a standard of behavior for God's people regarding ceremonial matters of formal worship as well as statutes for civil and social conduct.

The biblical notion of Torah conveys the sense of divinely authoritative instruction, which is different from our modern idea of law as a body of codes crafted and enacted by legislators. And it doesn't equate to our notions of "natural" law, which is discovered in nature rather than revealed by God.

 *Food for Thought*

What is the difference between the English word *law* and the Hebrew meaning of Torah? In what way does this assist you to see what was really happening between God and the Israelites? If it is not yet clear, what is confusing to you?

_____

_____

_____

_____

_____

_____

In Exodus, it is clear that Torah in the sense of a set of specific instructions is part of the covenant God makes with his people. The covenant describes the relationship that God has established between himself and his people by virtue of his act of deliverance on their behalf (Exod. 20:2). As the people's covenantal king, God then specifies how he desires Israel to worship and behave.

Israel's pledge to obey God is their *response* to God's gift of his covenant (Exod. 24:7). This is significant for our understanding of the theology of work. The way we discern God's will for our behavior at work, and the way we put that into practice in the workplace, flows from a relationship God established with us. In Christian terms, we love God because he first loved us, and we demonstrate that love in how we treat others (1 John 4:19–21). The categorical nature of God's command for us to love our neighbors means that God intends for us to apply it everywhere and in all that we do.

 *Food for Thought*

How could God's divinely authoritative instruction be a means
of God's love for us, rather than a demand for us to love God?

_____

_____

_____

_____

_____

_____

_____

Prayer

Pause for a few moments of silence to reflect on this lesson. Then
offer a prayer, either spontaneous or by using the following:

> *Lord,*
>
> *Thank you for the gift of your divinely authoritative in-
> struction. Although Christ has freed us from condemnation
> under the law, show us how to rejoice, as he did, that "not
> one stroke of a letter will pass from the law until all is
> accomplished." Help us to open our hearts to your Spirit
> in order to hear and live according to your Torah, so we
> might reflect your love in our workplaces.*
>
> *Amen.*

Lesson #2: The Role of the Law for Christians—Part 1 (Exodus 20:1–24:18)

It can be a challenge for a Christian to pull a verse from the book of Exodus, or especially Leviticus, and understand how that lesson should be applied today. Anyone who tries this should be prepared for the comeback, "Sure, but the Bible also permits slavery and says we can't eat bacon or shrimp! Plus, I don't think God really cares if my clothes are a cotton-polyester blend" (Exod. 21:2–11; Lev. 11:7, 12, and 19:19, respectively).

These responses are common enough within Christian circles, so we should not be surprised to find difficulties when applying the Bible to the subject of work in the public sphere. How can we know what applies today and what doesn't? How do we avoid the charge of inconsistency in our handling of the Bible? More importantly, how do we let God's word truly transform us in every area of life?

 Food for Thought

What are three Torah items in Exodus 22–23 that puzzle you in applying to your particular location and time in history? Discuss the interpretative method you usually apply to these passages.

_____

_____

_____

_____

_____

_____

_____

The New Testament's relationship to the law is complex. While Jesus says that "not one letter, not one stroke of a letter, will pass from the law" (Matt. 5:18), Paul states that "we are discharged from the law . . . not under the old written code but in the new life of the Spirit" (Rom. 7:6). These are not two opposing statements, but two ways of saying a common reality—that Torah continues to reveal God's gift of justice, wisdom, and inner transformation to those he has brought to new life in Christ.

Prayer

Pause for a few moments of silence to reflect on this lesson. Then offer a prayer, either spontaneous or by using the following:

> *Lord,*
>
> *When we read the instructions to the Israelites about making reparations for damage done by a runaway ox, or for the punishment of a man for stealing, we know that this is an expression of your overall concern for justice and equity in our communities. Grant that we might take to heart the wisdom found in the Torah and apply it appropriately to the way we conduct ourselves at work.*
>
> *Amen.*

Lesson #3: The Role of the Law for Christians—Part 2 (Exodus 20:1–24:18)

It becomes apparent that applying the Torah needs careful thought. Obeying the Torah by applying it to the issues of our contemporary life is *not* about a religious repetition of behaviors relevant only to the agrarian society of Israel thousands of years ago. We find indications that parts of the law were not intended to be permanent. For example, the tabernacle was temporary (Lev. 1:50–51), and Israel's enemies eventually destroyed their temple (2 Kings 25:15–17). Also, when Jesus said that it is not what goes into us that makes us unclean, he "declared all foods clean" (Mark 7:18–19), suggesting that the specific food laws of the Torah were no longer in force.

In New Testament times, the people of God lived in various countries where they had no legal authority to apply the instructions of the Torah. When the apostles considered such issues, guided by the Holy Spirit, they decided that many particulars of the Jewish law did not have to apply to Gentile Christians (Acts 15:28–29).

When asked which commandments were most important, Jesus gave an answer completely consistent with the Torah: "Love the Lord your God with all your heart, and with all your soul, and with all your mind, and with all your strength" and "Love your neighbor as yourself" (Mark 12:30–31). Much more in the New Testament confirms the Torah—not just in its negative commands against adultery, murder, theft, and coveting—but especially in its positive command to love one another (Rom. 13:8–10; Gal. 5:14).

According to Timothy Keller, "The coming of Christ changed how we worship, but not how we live." This is not surprising because in promising a New Covenant, God said he would put his law within his people and write it on their hearts (Jer. 31:33; Luke 22:20). Israel's faithfulness to the laws of the Mosaic covenant depended on *their willingness* to obey them, and in this they repeatedly failed. Ultimately, we recognize that only Jesus could accomplish this. Because of Jesus' obedience, new covenant believers have the privilege of a divine change of heart that frees us to be willing to obey the Torah. As Paul explained, "We serve in the new way of the Spirit" (Rom. 7:6 NIV).

Food for Thought

What do you think is the difference between new covenant obedience to the Torah and obedience to the Mosaic covenant?
How does that affect the way you apply the Torah to your work
situation?

_____

_____

_____

_____

_____

_____

_____

For Christians, the regulation of our behavior flows from allowing the transformation of our attitudes, motives, and desires by
the Holy Spirit (Rom. 12:1–2). Anything less than submission
to a change of heart amounts to avoidance of God's work and
will. The challenge from Christ is to allow *his* love to guide our
policies and behaviors.

 *Food for Thought*

How has God worked in your life to change your heart? How has this affected your life at work?

_____

_____

_____

_____

_____

_____

_____

_____

Prayer

Pause for a few moments of silence to reflect on this lesson. Then offer a prayer, either spontaneous or by using the following:

Lord,

When we come to faith in Christ, you give us a change of heart that upends our self-justification and opposition to your will. We long for this change so we can be more obedient to carry into our workplaces your love for your creation and the work of redeeming it.

Amen.

Chapter 5

A Proper Relationship with God

Israel's "Book of the Covenant" (Exod. 24:7) consists of the Ten Commandments (Exod. 20:1–17) and the "ordinances" (Exod. 21:1–23:19). The commandments are general commands either to do or not do something. The ordinances are a collection of case laws, applying the values of the Decalogue in specific situations using an "if . . . then" format. These case laws fit the socioeconomic world of ancient Israel. They are not exhaustive, but they function as templates for curbing the worst of human behavior and set legal precedent for difficult cases.

Because the Ten Commandments are the supreme expression of God's will in the Old Testament, and because Jesus and the writers of the New Testament affirmed them, we need to pay them close attention.

Lesson #1: "You Shall Have No Other Gods before Me" (Exodus 20:2–3)

Immediately, we are reminded that everything in the Torah flows from our responding to God in love for the love he has poured out on us. For Israel, this love was demonstrated by God's deliverance "out of the house of slavery" in Egypt (Exod. 20:2). Here, God directs us to make primary our desire to love and be loved by him. To place something else above our love for God is not so much breaking God's rules as a rejection of a relationship with him. Any other desire—money, power, security, recognition, sex, or anything else—can become our god. This god will have its own demands in opposition to God's, and we will inevitably violate the Torah as we comply with its requirements. Observing the Ten Commandments is conceivable only by desiring no other god than the one true God. As David Gill writes, "Never allow anyone or anything to threaten God's central place in your life." Because many people work primarily to make money, an inordinate desire for money is probably the most common work-related danger to the first commandment. "No one can serve two masters. . . . You cannot serve God and wealth" (Matt. 6:24).

Work-related benefits can seduce us to the point that they diminish our love for God. How many careers end tragically because the original means to accomplish something for the love of God—such as political power, financial stability, commitment to the job, status among peers, or superior performance—become ends in themselves? And when recognition on the job becomes more important than character on the job, isn't it a signal that reputation is displacing the love of God as the ultimate concern?

 Food for Thought

What is the significance to your work that God commands you to desire him first and foremost? What difference does it make to you that this is not so much a rule as it is the only means of developing a relationship with him?

John the Apostle gives us a touchstone for assessing our love for God on the job. It has to do with our relationship to others: "Those who say, 'I love God,' and hate their brothers or sisters, are liars; for those who do not love a brother or sister whom they have seen, cannot love God whom they have not seen. The commandment we have from him is this: those who love God must love their brothers and sisters also" (1 John 4:20–21).

If we put our individual concerns ahead of our concern for those around us, we have made our individual concerns our god. If we treat other people as things to be manipulated, obstacles to overcome, instruments to obtain what we want, or simply neutral objects in our field of view, we demonstrate that we do not love God with all our heart, soul, and mind.

 Food for Thought

What are some work-related behaviors and cultural norms with a high potential to interfere with our love for God? Do you have to deal with this in your own work? If so, how?

_____

_____

_____

_____

_____

_____

_____

Prayer

Pause for a few moments of silence to reflect on this lesson. Then offer a prayer, either spontaneous or by using the following:

Lord,

We experience many distractions from the primary desire to love you and be loved by you. Our work situations are rife with racism, verbal violence, jealousy, manipulation, political backstabbing, and other ills of human nature. The rewards offered for inordinate time and attention given to profit-making and other fruits of the job are seductive. We know we can't battle these forces alone. Help us to stand firm in the support of others and in the presence of your Spirit in the midst of doing work you want us to enjoy.

Amen.

Lesson #2: "You Shall Not Make for Yourself an Idol" (Exodus 20:4–6)

Idols are gods of our own creation—gods we design, gods we feel we control. Historically, idols have a physical representation. But the issue is really one of trust and devotion. On what do we ultimately pin our hope of well-being and success? Anything that is not capable of fulfilling our hope—that is, anything other than God—is an idol, whether or not it is a physical object.

 *Food for Thought*

One strategy for unmasking our work idols is to look at the "if only" items in our lives. Often they are quite legitimate desires. What do you feel you need in order for your life or career to be complete? How can you place this desire into harmony with the second commandment?

_____

_____

_____

_____

_____

_____

In the work world, money, fame, and power are universally regarded as potential idols. Although we may use work, money, fame, and power to accomplish our roles in God's creative and redemptive work in the world, we need to be careful. If we begin to imagine that we have ultimate control over them, or that our safety and prosperity will be secured by them, we have begun to fall into idolatry. This is also a pattern with other forms of achievement that involve preparation, hard work, creativity, risk, wealth and other resources, and favorable circumstances.

While we should recognize their importance, as God's people we especially need to identify when they begin to seduce us as idols. By God's grace, we can overcome the temptation to worship these things that are good in their own right. The development of genuinely godly wisdom and skill for any task is "so that your trust may be in the Lord" (Prov. 22:19).

 *Food for Thought*

What are two areas of work where you feel drawn to inordinate achievement? How have you managed these desires, or what grace have you seen working in your life here?

_____

_____

_____

_____

_____

_____

The distinctive element of idolatry is the man-made nature of the idol. At work, the danger arises when we mistake our power, knowledge, and opinions for an ultimate reality. For example, when a business promises a delivery date for a new product—without good evidence it can meet that date, and without informing the customer of the risks—the company has put its faith in a myth of its own making. Then its failure to deliver on time can really hurt its clients.

When employers use their own prejudices and projections to draw unsubstantiated conclusions about employees, have they not begun "a work of delusion" (Jer. 10:15)? In the strictest sense, these may not be violations of the second commandment, since they are offenses against people rather than against God himself. But when we remember that Jesus said, "As you did it to one of the least of these who are members of my family, you did it to me" (Matt. 25:40), we might let the second commandment remind us not to let our own devices and desires become the source of our values at work.

 *Food for Thought*

Although the consequences of idolatry fall on business clients and workers, in what way do you think the examples above also illustrate a rejection of God?

_____

_____

_____

_____

Prayer

Pause for a few moments of silence to reflect on this lesson. Then offer a prayer, either spontaneous or by using the following:

Lord,

We are left in awe that you have designed all things well and for your own purposes. We know that through heeding your commandments, we experience your glory and can enjoy you forever. Help us to desire that more than any promised benefit people offer to us. Give us the wisdom to discern when to accept the fruits of our work and govern them by the priorities of your law.

Amen.

Lesson #3: "You Shall Not Make Wrongful Use of the Name of the Lord Your God" (Exodus 20:7)

The third commandment plainly forbids God's people from making "wrongful use" of the name of God, which includes every name by which we identify our Triune God. But what is meant by "wrongful use"? Beyond the obvious—cursing, slandering, and blaspheming God—it includes falsely attributing human designs to God. We should not permit ourselves to attribute direct authority from God for our decisions and actions.

We have probably all experienced someone claiming divine sanction for their opinions as an excuse for dismissing other people's views. Perhaps we have done it ourselves. "God says that . . ." sounds blasphemous or simply deluded in the ears of others. Can we really claim to be speaking for God? "It is God's will that . . . ," or "God is punishing you for . . . ," are very dangerous things to say, and almost never valid when spoken by an individual without the discernment of the community of faith (1 Thess. 5:20–21). At the very least this suggests that we refrain from pronouncing God's views if we have not sought counsel from other believers in advance. In this light, perhaps the traditional Jewish reticence to utter even the English translation "God"—let alone the divine name itself—demonstrates a wisdom Christians often lack.

 Food for Thought

What has surprised you in the application of this third commandment? What are some ways we apply to ourselves the authority that belongs only to God? How does respect for his name help us avoid this arrogance?

_____

_____

_____

_____

_____

As is typical of all the commandments, the litmus test of application is in our actions affecting others. This third commandment also reminds us that respecting human names is important to God. The Good Shepherd "calls his own sheep by name" (John 10:3) while warning us that if you call another person "You fool," then "you will be liable to the hell of fire" (Matt. 5:22). Taking this to heart, we should shrink from the disrespectful use of other people's names. This can be blatant or subtle.

 Food for Thought

How have you experienced humiliation or seen it happen with others because of someone disrespecting your name or your co-worker? Have you done this yourself?

_____

_____

_____

_____

_____

_____

We use people's names well when we use their names to encourage, thank, create solidarity, and welcome. Simply to learn and say someone's name is a blessing, especially if he or she is often treated as nameless, invisible, or insignificant. Do you know the name of the person who empties your trashcan, answers your customer service call, or drives your bus? If these examples do not concern the very name of the Lord, they do concern the name of those made in his image.

 *Food for Thought*

How does respecting others in the workplace help fulfill the third commandment? Why?

_____

_____

_____

_____

_____

_____

_____

Prayer

Pause for a few moments of silence to reflect on this lesson. Then offer a prayer, either spontaneous or by using the following:

Lord,

Please forgive us for insulting your image when we utter disrespectful epithets, reduce others to caricatures, or fail to recognize the humanity of the people we work among. Please forgive us for our mindless disrespect, and help us to see the wonder and beauty of being named as your family.

Amen.

Chapter 6

Keeping the Sabbath, Respect for Parents, and Protection of Life

Lesson #1: "Remember the Sabbath Day, and Keep It Holy" (Exodus 20:8–11)

In the ancient world, only the nation of Israel took rest from its commerce one day in seven. But to keep this Sabbath required an extraordinary trust in God's provision. Six days of work had to be enough to plant crops, gather the harvest, carry water, spin cloth, and draw sustenance from creation. While Israel rested that one day every week, the surrounding nations continued to trade, forge swords, feather arrows, and train soldiers. Israel had to trust God not to let a day of rest lead to economic and military catastrophe.

The Sabbath is a complex institution, not only in the book of Exodus and the Old Testament, but also in Christian theology and practice. The first part of the command calls for ceasing labor one day in seven. In Exodus 16, it is mentioned in regard to gathering manna. It appears again as dealing with a seventh-year rest and the purpose of weekly rest (Exod. 23:10–12), and then deals with the penalty for violation (Exod. 31:12–17; 34:21; 35:1–3).

Food for Thought

Trust in God's provision is as much an issue for us today as it was for ancient Israel. How do you deal with the inherent tensions over your work in keeping Sabbath rest?

_____

_____

_____

_____

_____

_____

_____

_____

The fourth commandment simply tells us to rest one day in every seven, without a promise of blessing. Christians have instituted the day of rest on the Lord's Day (Sunday, the day of Christ's resurrection), but the essence of the Sabbath is not choosing one particular day of the week over another (Rom. 14:5–6). The real polarity that undergirds the Sabbath is *work* and *rest*. Both are included in the fourth commandment. The six days of work are as much a part of the commandment as the one day of rest.

So we find two pitfalls in the practice of the Sabbath: we can allow work to swallow up the time set aside for rest, or we can shirk our work for a life of leisure and dissipation. Both extremes are idolatrous and affect all our relationships. The Apostle Paul warns the lazy that "whoever does not provide for relatives, and especially for family members, has denied the faith and is worse than an unbeliever" (1 Tim. 5:8).

We need to develop a rhythm of work and rest, which is good for us, our family, workers, and guests. The rhythm may or may not include twenty-four continuous hours of rest falling on a Sunday (or a Saturday). What's important is taking this rest.

 Food for Thought

What kind of rhythm of rest from work have you developed or would like to develop? How do you sustain it or how can you implement it?

_____

_____

_____

_____

_____

_____

When the extremes of workaholism or sheer laziness endanger us, it is worthless to attempt to honor the Sabbath by instituting a false legalism of church attendance and rest that swings the pendulum far in the other direction against our tendencies. It is a false dichotomy to make a Sabbath day more important than our workday week, or vice versa. Regular Sabbath worship, hearing the word of God, and participating in the sacraments can lead us into deep reflection on the issues of our hearts. And diligently seeking answers in that context as to why we might mistakenly find our worth in our work, or why we avoid the responsibilities of meaningful work, will certainly be honored by Christ. He can restore the balance where we find joy and meaning in working as a service to God and our neighbors (Eph. 4:28).

Food for Thought

In regard to work and rest, toward which extreme are you drawn and how do you keep your balance? If you are off balance, what can you do to make it right?

_____

_____

_____

_____

_____

Prayer

Pause for a few moments of silence to reflect on this lesson. Then offer a prayer, either spontaneous or by using the following:

Lord,

Thank you for the privilege of the Sabbath with its rhythm of work and rest, which is patterned on the very rhythm of eternal life we have by your Holy Spirit. Grant that we might increasingly discover the joy of living by your Sabbath.

Amen.

Lesson #2: "Honor Your Father and Your Mother" (Exodus 20:12)

At first glance, this commandment might seem unrelated to our work. But for anyone with elderly, ill, or disabled parents, the connection is obvious. The command places the responsibility for their care and well-being on their children. Providing care, or earning money to pay for care, in these circumstances is work.

Regardless of our parents' health, we honor them when we take a job because it allows us to live near them, send money to them, make use of the values and gifts they developed in us, or accomplish what they taught us as important. We honor them when we limit our careers so that we can be present with them, clean and cook for them, bathe and embrace them, take them to the places they love, or diminish their fears.

When the Pharisees restricted "Honor your father and your mother" to simply speaking well of parents, Jesus overruled them. Obeying the fifth commandment requires the real work of meeting their needs (Mark 7:9–13). We honor people by working for their good, and we dishonor them when we pay them only lip service.

 Food for Thought

What thought have you given to this dimension of the commandment, or what experience have you had with your own parents that might illustrate Jesus' clarification of this law?

_____

_____

_____

_____

_____

_____

_____

For many people, good relationships with their parents are one of the joys of life. To love and serve them is a delight, and obeying this commandment is easy. But for Millie, the commandment tested her. When she was four years old, her alcoholic father abandoned her and her mother, and when he turned up in her adult life, it was for a handout. A decade had passed without further contact when he knocked on her door one evening, looking for lodging. He said he had terminal cancer and just wanted to see her. It was a hard call for Millie. She offered her home for just two nights and then sought guidance from one of her church elders.

After listening to her grief, the elder asked her what she wanted to do. Millie was conflicted but favored helping her dad, as it might help him to recognize the Lord she served. Her mentor agreed that she had everything to gain by honoring her ill father, as service to Christ, and that she might live with regret if she turned him away.

To her surprise, she and her father had frank talks with a feeling of normal affection between them. Her dad attempted an apology for his behavior. After a week, he returned to his own state where he died in the hospital shortly afterwards. Millie's sorrow at the consequence of his addiction was tempered by an inner joy. She had honored him with hospitality, not as a family obligation or for emotional payout, but in service to Christ.

She still speaks of the peaceful sense of blessing she has known since that time, which should not be a surprise as the fifth commandment comes with a promise: "that your days may be long in the land that the Lord your God is giving you."

 *Food for Thought*

Although it may be difficult to care for aging parents, many find it an unexpected blessing to honor them this way, even in difficult circumstances. What stories do you know in which honoring parents was arduous, long, and sacrificial, yet a blessing?

_____

_____

_____

_____

_____

_____

Lesson #3: "You Shall Not Murder" (Exodus 20:13)

Although job-related homicides aren't overly common, it does get our notice when such a tragedy occurs. But murder isn't the only form of workplace violence, just the most extreme. We gain a better perspective on the breadth of this command from Jesus who says that even anger is a violation of the sixth commandment (Matt. 5:21–22), and the Apostle Paul writes, "Be angry but do not sin; do not let the sun go down on your anger" (Eph. 4:26). We may not be able to prevent the feeling of anger, but we can learn how to cope with our anger.

 Food for Thought

How surprising is it that the command concerning murder includes dealing with its root, anger? What are the effects of anger that you have experienced in your workplace?

The most significant application of the sixth commandment for work then may be, "If you get angry at work, get help in anger management." Many employers, churches, state and local governments, and nonprofit organization offer classes and counseling in anger management, and availing oneself of these may be a highly effective way of obeying the sixth commandment.

Murder is the intentional killing of a person, but the case law that stems from the sixth commandment shows that we also have the duty to prevent unintended deaths. A particularly graphic case is when an ox (a work animal) gores a person to death (Exod. 21:28–29). If the event was predictable, the ox's owner is to be treated as a murderer. In other words, owners/managers are responsible for ensuring workplace safety where peoples' lives or physical well-being are clearly endangered.

This principle is well-established law in most Western countries whose legal systems were shaped in their formative years by biblical imperatives to care for others. And so, workplace safety is the subject of significant government policing, industry self-regulation, and organizational policy and practice. Yet workplaces of all kinds continue to require or allow workers to labor in needlessly unsafe conditions. Christians with roles in setting the conditions of work, supervising workers, or modeling workplace practices are reminded by the sixth commandment that safe working conditions are among their highest responsibilities in the world of work.

 *Food for Thought*

One of the greatest implications in all of the commandments is that we should take responsibility for our behavior. Name some examples of dangerous behavior at work that you have seen addressed or perhaps ignored. If you were the manager responsible, how would you (or how did you) go about addressing the need for safety?

_____

_____

_____

_____

_____

_____

_____

_____

Prayer

Pause for a few moments of silence to reflect on this lesson. Then offer a prayer, either spontaneous or by using the following:

Lord,

So often we overlook the value of people when we allow anger to go unchecked at work or when we overlook safety issues. Grant that we would watch carefully our own propensity to violence against others in our workplaces. Help us to safeguard the lives of all people at work.

Amen.

Chapter 7

Unfaithfulness, Theft, and False Witness

Lesson #1: "You Shall Not Commit Adultery" (Exodus 20:14)

The seventh commandment touches the electric nerve of faithfulness in marriage, and its shortness and sharpness express God's intention for it: an unbreakable covenant. In order to protect marriage, we have to value how it develops us to reflect the love relationship of the three persons of the Godhead—the inviolable unity of eternal love.

 Food for Thought

What protocols exist in your workplace to encourage faithfulness in marriage and discourage casual work-based liaisons? If none, how do you maintain for yourself a high view of marriage and the absolute nature of the commandment?

_____

_____

_____

_____

_____

_____

The workplace is a common setting for adultery, because of the amount of time we spend working with others, sometimes more intimately than with our spouses. People who travel for work— salespeople, musicians, journalists, field scientists, film crews, and so on—all know the emotional tug away from faithfulness to the spouse who is not sharing in the immediacy of the adventure. This also happens in hospitals, entrepreneurial ventures, academic institutions and, yes, even churches.

Some work cultures subject people to sexual harassment, especially from those with power to advance careers. Notoriety gained through work can inflate a person's ego or expose them to adulation that generates unfaithfulness. Work that requires close physical contact, or long hours of overtime—indeed any kind of work that sets up dynamics that erode the bonds of marriage—infringes on the seventh commandment.

 Food for Thought

If you are married, what dynamics at work put pressure on your marriage? How do you deal with this? If you are single, what kind of culture exists in your workplace regarding marriage?

_____

_____

_____

_____

_____

Since these kinds of pressures are common in the diversity of human work, we need to be realistic about the temptations that will occur and consider strategies that maintain the highest view of Christian marriage. From that certainty we can develop behavioral norms for ourselves that maintain our own faithfulness and encourage others in theirs.

It requires a rare honesty in self-awareness to know one's weaknesses and strengths. Some people may know that it is wise for them to avoid jobs entailing emotional or physical temptation toward adultery. Others may regard the pitfalls as obstacles to be negotiated for the necessary nature of the work, and create for themselves accountability structures that link them to faithful friends.

The distinctive aspect of a covenant violated by adultery is that it is a covenant with *God* that we break, that we are rejecting who he is. Paul exhorts us, "Whatever you do, in word or deed, do everything in the name of the Lord Jesus" (Col. 3:17). Let us honor all our agreements and encourage others to honor theirs. Whether this is contained in Exodus 20:14 or expounded in the Old and New Testament teachings that arise from it, "Keep your promises, and help others keep theirs," may serve as a practical definition of the seventh commandment in the world of work.

 Food for Thought

Those who are married and who are concerned about infidelity should keep themselves accountable to others. What else can be done in the workplace to avoid this temptation?

_____

_____

_____

_____

_____

Prayer

Pause for a few moments of silence to reflect on this lesson. Then offer a prayer, either spontaneous or by using the following:

> *Lord,*
>
> *Make us aware of our own desires, and give us the gift of accountability to others as we manage our own behavior. Keep us alert to influences that tempt us to excuse unfaithfulness or erode the covenant of marriage. Give us the resources to keep our promises and encourage others to do the same.*
>
> *Amen.*

Lesson #2: "You Shall Not Steal" (Exodus 20:15)

Stealing is a violation of honest work because it takes from the victims the fruits of their labor. The terseness of this command underlines the significance of the Sabbath command on work and rest, since stealing is usually an attempted end-run around the requirement of work.

Any time we acquire something of value from its rightful owner without consent, we are engaging in theft. Misappropriating corporate resources or funds for personal use is stealing. Using deception to make sales, gain market share, or raise prices is stealing because information a buyer needs to make a wise choice is withheld or distorted. (See the section on "Puffery/ Exaggeration" in Truth and Deception at www.theologyofwork .org for more on this topic.)

Profiting by taking advantage of people's fears, vulnerabilities, powerlessness, or desperation is a form of stealing because their consent is not truly voluntary. Violating patents, copyrights, and other intellectual property laws is stealing because it deprives the owners of being able to profit from their creation under the terms of civil law.

Sadly, many jobs seem to include an element of taking advantage of others' ignorance or lack of alternatives to lure them into transactions they otherwise wouldn't agree to. In addition, companies, governments, individuals, unions, and other players may use their power to coerce others into unfair wages, prices, financial terms, working conditions, hours, or other factors.

Although we may not rob banks, steal from our employers, or shoplift, we may be participating in unfair or unethical practices that deprive others of what is rightfully theirs. It can be difficult, even career-limiting, to resist engaging in these practices, but we are called to do so nonetheless.

 Food for Thought

Recently, many companies in the financial industry marketed bundles of U.S. mortgages as securities that were high risk, in many cases to people who did not understand the high risk. Did this practice violate the command not to steal? What do you think was the responsibility of the salespeople who understood the risk inherent in the packages? Are there deceptive practices in your line of work? If so, what are they and what can you do about them?

_____

_____

_____

_____

_____

Lesson #3: "You Shall Not Bear False Witness against Your Neighbor" (Exodus 20:16)

The ninth commandment protects a person's reputation from the malice of others. It finds pointed application in legal proceedings in which personal testimony may determine the course of lives. When judges and juries decide an issue on false evidence, it can send an innocent person to death row or cost another their livelihood. When the ethical fabric of society is torn, there is a disintegration of trust in the institutions that are supposed to reward good and punish evil. Walter Brueggemann says this commandment recognizes "that community life is not possible unless there is an arena in which there is public confidence that social reality will be reliably described and reported."

We should never say or do anything that misrepresents someone else. In this light, we can see that workplace gossip is as serious an offense as false testimony or deceptive advertising. As Christians, we must refuse to participate in or to tolerate any conversation in which a person is being defamed or accused without the person being there to give a defense. It could be in a prayer meeting as much as in a courtroom, at a business meeting, or on the beach.

What is necessary on a personal level is of similar importance among institutions. For example, the business of marketing and advertising operates in the public space. How ethical is it for a company to present its own products and services in the best possible light, and then point out the flaws and weaknesses of a competing product or service without incorporating the other company's perspective? Is it possible that the rights of "your neighbor" could include the rights of other companies?

In a global economy, this command has wide application. Where perception often counts for reality, the rhetoric of effective persuasion may or may not have much to do with the truth. The divine origin of this command reminds us that whatever people think about our representation of others, God is never fooled. Yes, it's good to do the right thing when nobody is watching. But with this command, we understand that we must speak truthfully, whoever is listening. (See "Truth and Deception" at www .theologyofwork.org for a much fuller discussion of this topic, including whether the prohibition of "false witness against your neighbor" includes all forms of lying and deception.)

 Food for Thought

What subtleties of deception are you aware of in your own workplace that amount to lying? How do you deal with them?

_____

_____

_____

_____

_____

Prayer

Pause for a few moments of silence to reflect on this lesson. Then offer a prayer, either spontaneous or by using the following:

Lord,

Have mercy on us for the way we use our tongues. Help us to be those who protect the reputations of others, rather than those who cast doubt on them or self-righteously denounce them. When we feel we must speak negatively of another person, give us the courage and respect to do so only in their presence and to be open to their response.

Amen.

Chapter 8

Coveting, Slavery, and Commercial Restitution

Lesson #1: "You Shall Not Covet . . . Anything that Belongs to Your Neighbor" (Exodus 20:17)

We are most likely to envy those people we regard as like us in ability and achievement. With them it's easiest to make comparisons and believe that their good fortune is in some ways at the cost of our own. At work we may not be able to relate to the lifestyle of a Fortune 500 CEO, but it's a different experience when we see the perks or the successes of our immediate bosses or colleagues.

We may come to envy the status, pay, and power of these people or people we know in other social contexts. While there are many good reasons to desire achievement, advancement, or reward at work, envy of others isn't one of them. Added to that, the acquisition of socially recognized symbols of "success" is just as dangerous as a motivation. A crop of car television commercials trade on people looking with envy at our new ride, wondering why they haven't the same good fortune. It is saying, "Isn't it fun to be the ones who are envied for choosing this car!" But envy isn't fun, and it can lead to unwise and unethical behavior (James 4:2–4).

 *Food for Thought*

What are good reasons to desire achievement, advancement, and reward at work? What experiences can you relate that demonstrate the subtle infiltration of envy and acquisitiveness into a person's motivation?

_____

_____

_____

_____

_____

_____

_____

We can face temptation at work to falsely inflate our accomplishments at the expense of others. The antidote is as simple as it is hard to do. We need to make it a consistent practice to recognize the accomplishments of others and give them all the credit they deserve. If we can learn to rejoice in—or at least acknowledge—others' successes, then we cut off the source of envy and covetousness at work, and celebrate each person's unique giftedness. Such an attitude actually assists us to appreciate our own unique giftedness, which also allows us to better focus our work efforts. If we can learn how to work so that our success goes hand-in-hand with others' success, then covetousness is replaced by collaboration and envy by unity.

Food for Thought

If you have been praised at work or in other situations, what did it mean to you? How did it change your perception of the person who offered the compliment? How did it change your perception of yourself?

_____

_____

_____

_____

_____

_____

_____

Prayer

Pause for a few moments of silence to reflect on this lesson. Then offer a prayer, either spontaneous or by using the following:

> *Lord,*
>
> *Grant that we might be grateful for every good gift that comes from you and honor your provision to others as well. Help us to turn over to you our envy and covetousness so that our work with others becomes a joy of collaborative endeavor.*
>
> *Amen.*

At this point, the Ten Commandments come to a close. Exodus then explores a collection of case laws flowing from the Ten Commandments. Instead of developing detailed principles, the collection gives examples of how to apply God's law to the kinds of situations in the conduct of daily life. As cases, they are all embedded in the circumstances faced by the people of Israel. Indeed, throughout the Pentateuch (the Torah), it can be difficult to sift out the specific laws from the surrounding narrative and exhortation. Four sections of the case law are particularly applicable to work today, which we will now explore.

Lesson #2: Slavery or Indentured Servitude (Exodus 21:1–11)

Although God liberated the Hebrews from slavery in Egypt, slavery is not universally prohibited in the Bible. Slavery was permissible in certain situations, so long as slaves were regarded as full members of the community (Gen. 17:12), received the same rest periods and holidays as free persons (Exod. 23:12; Deut. 5:14–15; 12:12), and were treated humanely (Exod. 21:7; 26–27). Cruelty on the part of the owner was to result in immediate freedom for the slave (Exod. 21:26–27). These restrictions made slavery in ancient Israel significantly different from the absolute or "chattel" slavery practiced in the Western world until recent times.

Most importantly, slavery was not intended as a permanent condition, but a voluntary, temporary refuge for people suffering what would otherwise be desperate poverty. "When you buy a male Hebrew slave, he shall serve six years, but in the seventh he shall go out a free person, without debt" (Exod. 21:2). This made Hebrew slavery more like a long-term labor contract among individuals, and less like the kind of permanent racial/class/ethnic exploitation familiar to us today. This is not to make light of the conditions of slavery in ancient Israel, but only to note that they were different from what we know as slavery today.

 *Food for Thought*

What differences do you see between slavery in the ancient world and slavery in the world today? Do Christians have a greater imperative to fight against modern sex trafficking, forced labor, and worker exploitation?

_____

_____

_____

_____

_____

_____

The general equality between slave owners and slaves is highlighted by the regulations about female slaves in Exodus 21:7–11. The only purpose contemplated for buying a female slave was so that she could become the wife of either the buyer or the buyer's son (Exod. 21:8–9). She became the social equal (as wife) of the slaveholder, and the purchase functioned much like the giving of a dowry. Indeed, she is even called a "wife" by the regulation (Exod. 21:9). Moreover, if the buyer failed to treat the female slave with all the rights due an ordinary wife, he was required to set her free. "She shall go out without debt, without payment of money" (Exod. 21:11).

Despite these regulations, it appears that in some cases, girls or women were bought as wives for male slaves, rather than for the slave owner or a son, which resulted in a problematic situation (Exod. 21:4). This reminds us that slavery in ancient Israel was far from an ideal situation, and in its biblical setting was intended only as a respite in desperate circumstances.

Food for Thought

Are you aware of situations comparable today where workers are hired without respect to their dignity as persons? What about immigrant workers? How would you suggest their employment could be negotiated in a godly way?

_____

_____

_____

_____

_____

By no means was slavery an agreeable way of life. Slaves were, for the duration of their enslavement, property. Whatever the regulations, in practice there was probably little protection against maltreatment, and abuses occurred. The safeguards for foreign-born slaves were not as stringent as for Hebrews (Lev. 25:44–46) and, as noted above, protections for women were less than for men.

As in much of the Bible, God's law in Exodus did not create a new form of social and economic organization, but it did instruct God's people how to live with justice and compassion in their circumstances. To our eyes, the results do—and should—appear disquieting.

Yet we can't be smug. The working conditions that prevail among poor people in every corner of the world, including developed nations, cry out for our attention. People work ceaselessly in two or three jobs to support families. They endure abuse at the hands of those in power. The fruits of their labor are confiscated by illicit business operators, corrupt officials, and politically connected bosses.

 *Food for Thought*

If it was God's will to protect Israel from exploitation even in slavery, what does God expect followers of Christ to do for those who suffer the same oppression, and worse, today? What difference can you make in your workplace or in your community?

_____

_____

_____

_____

_____

_____

_____

Prayer

Pause for a few moments of silence to reflect on this lesson. Then offer a prayer, either spontaneous or by using the following:

Lord,

How easily we disrespect our forebears for the way they constructed their societies. But when we look at the ills affecting our contemporary world, it's like observing the speck in the eye of the other and missing the beam in our own. Help us to embody your intention for the world as revealed in your word.

Amen.

Lesson #3: Commercial Restitution (Exodus 21:18–22:15)

The ordinances for ethical conduct spelled out penalties for offenses, including many relating to commerce, especially in the case of liability for loss or injury. *Lex talionis* ("the law of retaliation"), which also appears in Leviticus 24:17–21 and Deuteronomy 19:16–21, is central to the concept of retribution. The law says to repay a life for a life that is taken, an eye for an eye, a tooth for tooth, a hand for hand, a foot for foot, a burn for burn, a wound for wound, and a bruise for bruise (Exod. 21:23–25). The list is notably specific.

When Israel's judges did their work, are we really to believe they applied punishments in this way? Would a plaintiff who was burned due to someone's negligence really be satisfied to see the offender literally burned to the same degree? Interestingly, in this very part of Exodus, we do not see the *lex talionis* being applied in this manner. Instead, a man who seriously injures another in a fight must pay for the victim's lost time and cover his medical expenses (Exod. 21:19). The text does not say he must sit still for a public, comparable beating by his former victim.

It appears that the *lex talionis* did not determine the standard penalty for major offenses, but that it set an upper ceiling for damages that could be claimed. Gordon Wenham notes, "In Old Testament times there were no police or public prosecution services, so all prosecution and punishment had to be carried out by the injured party and his family. Thus it would be quite possible for injured parties not to insist on their full rights under the *lex talionis*, but negotiate a lower settlement or even forgive the offender altogether." This law may be perceived by some today as savage, but as Alec Motyer observes, "When English law hanged a person for stealing a sheep, it was not because the principle of 'an eye for an eye' was being practiced, but because it had been forgotten." Even today, the law is sometimes harsher than the biblical *lex talionis*. Commercial law in the United States sometimes mandates treble damages, for instance. Disproportionately long prison sentences for selected drug crimes might also be seen as an example.

 Food for Thought

In Jesus' teaching in Matthew 5:38–42, was he speaking of a personal ethic, or did he expect his followers to apply this principle in business, government, and other spheres of work? Does it make a difference whether the offense in question is small or large?

_____

_____

_____

_____

_____

_____

The specific instructions about restitution and penalties for thievery accomplished two aims. First, they made thieves responsible for returning the original owners to their original state or fully compensating them for their loss. Second, they punished and educated thieves by causing them to experience the full pain they had caused the victim. These aims can form a Christian basis for the work of civil and criminal law today.

Judicial work today operates according to specific statutes and guidelines set by the state. But even so, judges have a measure of freedom to set sentences and penalties. For disputes that are settled out of court, attorneys negotiate to help their clients reach a conclusive agreement. In recent times, a perspective called "restorative justice" has emerged with an emphasis on punishment that restores the victim's original condition and, to the extent possible, restores the perpetrator as a productive member of society. A full description and assessment of such approaches is beyond our scope here, but the Scripture has much to offer contemporary systems of justice in this regard.

 Food for Thought

In your own words, how does the aim of the *lex talionis* find application in our modern workplace laws?

_____

_____

_____

_____

_____

_____

_____

In business, leaders sometimes must mediate between workers who have serious work-related issues with each other. Deciding the right and fair thing affects not only the ones embroiled in the dispute, but also the atmosphere of the whole organization. It may even serve to set a precedent for how workers may expect to fare in the future. The immediate stakes may be high. On top of this, when Christians must make these kinds of decisions, onlookers draw conclusions about us as people, as well as about the legitimacy of the faith we claim to live by. Clearly, we cannot anticipate every situation (and neither does the book of Exodus). But we do know that God expects us to apply his instructions, and we can be confident that asking God how to love our neighbors as ourselves is the best place to start.

 Food for Thought

How do your own experiences of workplace justice accord with Christian application of the Torah? If they don't accord, what can you do differently?

_____

_____

_____

_____

_____

_____

Prayer

Pause for a few moments of silence to reflect on this lesson. Then offer a prayer, either spontaneous or by using the following:

> *Lord,*
>
> *Once again we are looking for the appropriate application of this ordinance. Help us to find the balance of proper restitution and proportional punishment in dealing with misbehavior in our workplace. Help us to care enough to seek what is just, according to the Torah.*
>
> *Amen.*

Chapter 9

Additional Case Laws in the Book of the Covenant

Lesson #1: Productive Opportunities for the Poor (Exodus 22:21–27; 23:10–11)

Exodus demonstrates God's concern to provide benefits for aliens, widows, and orphans (Exod. 22:21–22)—all of whom lacked land on which to support themselves, which is why they are synonyms for poverty in the Old Testament.

In Deuteronomy, God's concern for these vulnerable people called for Israel to give them access to justice (Deut. 10:18; 27:19) and the opportunity to feed themselves (Deut. 24:19–22). Case law on this matter is also developed in Isaiah 1:17, 23; 10:1–2; Jeremiah 5:28; 7:5–7; 22:3; Ezekiel 22:6–7; Zechariah 7:8–10; and Malachi 3:5.

One of the most important of these regulations is the practice of allowing the poor to harvest, or "glean," the leftover grain in active fields and to harvest all volunteer crops in fields lying fallow. The practice of gleaning was not a handout, but an opportunity for the poor to work to support themselves. Landowners were required to leave each field, vineyard, and orchard fallow one year in every seven, and the poor were allowed to harvest anything that might grow there during that time (Exod. 23:10–11).

Even in active fields, owners were to leave some of the grain in the field for the poor to harvest, rather than stripping the field bare (Lev. 19:9–10). For example, an olive grove or a vineyard was to be harvested only once each season (Deut. 24:20). After that, the poor were entitled to gather what was left over, perhaps what was of lesser quality or slower to ripen. This practice was not only an expression of kindness, but it was also a matter of justice. The book of Ruth revolves around gleaning to enchanting effect (see "Ruth 2:17–23" in "Ruth and Work" and "Exodus 22:21–27" in "Exodus and Work" at www.theologyofwork.org).

 Food for Thought

Who are the vulnerable in our urban society (the aliens, widows, and orphans of today)? What are ways businesses can provide opportunities to such as these?

_____

_____

_____

_____

_____

_____

_____

With training and support, people from disadvantaged backgrounds, prisoners returning to society, and others who have difficulty finding conventional employment can become productive workers and earn a living. Other economically vulnerable people may have to depend for a time on contributions of money instead of receiving opportunities to work. Here again the modern situation is too complex for us to proclaim a simplistic application of the biblical law.

But the values underlying the law may offer a significant contribution to the design and execution of systems of public welfare, personal charity, and corporate social responsibility. Many Christians have significant roles in hiring workers or designing employment policies. Exodus reminds us that employing vulnerable workers is an essential part of what it means for people to live under God's covenant. We have experienced God's redemption through Christ Jesus in our own unique contexts. Gratitude for his grace expressed through his church is historically the motivator for the societies that care for their marginal people. It applies to workplace culture as well.

 Food for Thought

What unique opportunity exists in your business or workplace for employing "aliens, widows, and orphans"? If they don't already exist, what can you do to create such opportunities?

_____

_____

_____

_____

_____

_____

Prayer

Pause for a few moments of silence to reflect on this lesson. Then offer a prayer, either spontaneous or by using the following:

> *Lord,*
>
> *We often blame poor people for their own predicaments and neglect to provide them with a helping hand. Help us to have hearts and minds open to create work opportunities in our lines of work for people in need.*
>
> *Amen.*

Lesson #2: Lending and Collateral (Exodus 22:25–27)

Another set of case laws regulated money and collateral (Exod. 22:25–27), and two situations are in view. The first pertains to needy members of God's people who require a financial loan, which should not be made according to the usual standards of money-lending. It should be given without "interest."

The Hebrew word *neshekh* deals with interest charged, and without *neshekh* always pertains to lending to those who are in miserable and vulnerable circumstances, for whom paying any interest at all would be an inescapable burden. Placing the poor into a never-ending cycle of financial indebtedness has always stirred Israel's compassionate God to action.

Whether or not this law was good for business is not in view here. Providing financial assistance to those in need is a situation outside the normal business of commercial finance, making it a responsibility of the community as a whole, including the financial sector. Walter Brueggemann notes, "The law does not argue about the economic viability of such a practice. It simply requires the need for care in concrete ways, and it expects the community to work out the practical details."

 Food for Thought

How does it affect your view of lending to the poor to realize it is not meant to be "economically viable"? Where is the burden of its cost meant to lie?

_____

_____

_____

_____

_____

_____

The other situation envisages a man who puts up his only coat as collateral for a loan. It should be returned to him at night so he can sleep without endangering his health (Exod. 22:26–27). Does this mean that the creditor should visit him in the morning to collect the coat for the day and to keep doing so until the loan is repaid? In the context of such obvious destitution, a godly creditor could avoid the near absurdity of this cycle by simply not expecting the borrower to put up any collateral at all.

Bankruptcy laws, which provide relief to people with unpayable debts, are a modern application of this principle. Another is microfinance, a new industry in less developed countries tailored to meet the needs of poor people who otherwise have no access to credit. The goal is not to maximize profit for the lenders, but to provide sustainable lending institutions to help the poor escape poverty. Even so, microfinance struggles with balancing the lenders' need for a sustainable return with the borrowers' need for affordable interest rates and nonrestrictive collateral terms.

 Food for Thought

If caring for the poor sometimes means suspending normal banking practices, what kind of alliance of agencies might be needed to achieve the goal of providing collateral-free loans and yet sustainable lending? Would you be willing to invest some of your savings in this kind of enterprise, knowing that the return would be less than if you invested in ordinary financial instruments?

———————————————————————————

———————————————————————————

———————————————————————————

———————————————————————————

———————————————————————————

The presence of specific regulations following the Ten Commandments means that God wants his people to honor him by putting his instructions into actual practice to serve real needs. Studying the specific applications of these laws in ancient Israel helps us to think about the particular ways we can act today. But we remember that even then these cases were illustrations. Terence Fretheim concludes, "There is an open-endedness to the application of the law. The text invites the hearer/reader to extend this passage out into every sphere of life where injustice might be encountered. In other words, one is invited by the law to go beyond the law."

A careful reading reveals three reasons why God's people should keep these laws and apply them to fresh situations. First, the Israelites themselves were oppressed as foreigners in Egypt (Exod. 22:21; 23:9). Rehearsing this history not only keeps God's redemption in view, but memory also becomes a motivation to treat others as we would like to be treated (Matt. 7:12). Second, God hears the cry of the oppressed and acts on it, especially when we won't (Exod. 22:22–25). Third, we are to be his holy people (Exod. 22:31; Lev. 19:2).

 Food for Thought

What does it mean to you that "one is invited by the law to go beyond the law"? How might this apply to making loans to situations in your workplace and community?

_____

_____

_____

_____

_____

Prayer

Pause for a few moments of silence to reflect on this lesson. Then offer a prayer, either spontaneous or by using the following:

Lord,

You are generous, and you want us also to live generously. Help us to make space in our economic lives for needy people so we can contribute to their well-being and express your own heart.

Amen.

Lesson #3: The Tabernacle (Exodus 25:1–27:21; 40:1–38)

The book of Exodus does not separate Israel's life into categories such as the "sacred" and "secular" divisions that we are accustomed to. The building of the tabernacle cannot be equated with "church work" today, but rather applies to all kinds of contemporary work. It was, after all, a work of art and a construction job.

The large section in Exodus about the tabernacle is organized according to God's command (Exod. 25:1–31:11) and Israel's response (Exod. 35:4–40:33). But God did more than tell Israel what he wanted from them. He provided the actual design for it. This is clear from his words to Moses, "In accordance with all that I show you concerning the pattern of the tabernacle and the pattern of all its furniture, so you shall make it" (Exod. 25:9).

From the descriptions that follow, it is clear that God's architectural design is exquisite and artful. The principle that God's design precedes God's building is true of Israel's sanctuaries, as well as the New Testament worldwide community of Christians (1 Cor. 3:5–18). The people of God may engage in their work (whatever it is) with the awareness that God also has a design for it.

 Food for Thought

In what way is God the designer of your particular field of work? What do you regard as his purpose for your industry?

_____

_____

_____

_____

_____

Bezalel, Oholiab, and all of the skilled workers on the tabernacle were engaged by God in a full range of craftsmanship and labor. The construction of the tabernacle required metalwork in gold, silver, and bronze, as well as stonework and woodwork (Exod. 31:1–11; 35:30–36:5). The fabrication of garments required obtaining wool and spinning, dyeing, weaving, and designing clothes, manufacturing and tailoring, and the work of embroidery. The craftsmen then prepared anointing oil and fragrant incense. What unites all of these practices is God filling the workers with his Spirit.

The Hebrew word for "ability" and "skill" in these texts (*hokhmah*) is usually translated as "wisdom," which causes us to think also about intellectual work and decision-making. It describes work that is clearly practical yet spiritual in the fullest theological sense (Exod. 28:3; 31:3, 6; 35:26, 31, 35; 36:1–2).

The wide range of construction activities in these passages illustrates, but does not exhaust, what building in the ancient Near East entailed. The Bible does not have to name every noble profession for us to see it as godly work. Just as people were not made for the Sabbath but the Sabbath for people (Mark 2:27), building and cities are made for people too. The law that ancient houses be built with a protective parapet around the flat roof (Deut. 22:8) illustrates God's concern for responsible construction that truly serves and protects people. Whatever God's work for each of us is, he equips us to do it with skilled hands.

 *Food for Thought*

How do you see God filling you with wisdom and skill as you work? Do you sense that you are fulfilling his designs in your work?

_____

_____

_____

_____

_____

_____

_____

_____

Prayer

Pause for a few moments of silence to reflect on this lesson. Then offer a prayer, either spontaneous or by using the following:

> Lord,
>
> *Thank you for giving us skill and wisdom for the work you call us to in every field of human endeavor. We long to experience your Spirit guiding us through the mundane tasks of every day, and for rejoicing with us in the exhilarating parts of our work. Come, Lord, and help us be faithful at our tasks, as we prepare for you to reveal your great city and our future home, where all that we have longed and worked for will be realized!*
>
> Amen.

Wisdom for Using This Study in the Workplace

Community within the workplace is a good thing and a Christian community within the workplace is even better. Sensitivity is needed, however, when we get together in the workplace (even a Christian workplace) to enjoy fellowship time together, learn what the Bible has to say about our work, and encourage one another in Jesus' name. When you meet at your place of employment, here are some guidelines to keep in mind:

- *Be sensitive to your surroundings.* Know your company policy about having such a group on company property. Make sure not to give the impression that this is a secret or exclusive group.

- *Be sensitive to time constraints.* Don't go over your allotted time. Don't be late to work! Make sure you are a good witness to the others (especially non-Christians) in your workplace by being fully committed to your work during working hours and doing all your work with excellence.

- *Be sensitive to the shy or silent members of your group.* Encourage everyone in the group and give them a chance to talk.

- *Be sensitive to the others by being prepared.* Read the Bible study material and Scripture passages and think about your answers to the questions ahead of time.

These Bible studies are based on the Theology of Work biblical commentary. Besides reading the commentary, please visit the Theology of Work website (www.theologyofwork.org) for videos, interviews, and other material on the Bible and your work.

Leader's Guide

Living Word. It is always exciting to start a new group and study. The possibilities of growth and relationship are limitless when we engage with one another and with God's word. Always remember that God's word is "alive and active, sharper than any double-edged sword" (Heb. 4:12) and when you study his word, it should change you.

A Way Has Been Made. Please know you and each person joining your study have been prayed for by people you will probably never meet but who share your faith. And remember that "the LORD himself goes before you and will be with you; he will never leave you nor forsake you. Do not be afraid; do not be discouraged" (Deut. 31:8). As a leader, you need to know that truth. Remind yourself of it throughout this study.

Pray. It is always a good idea to pray for your study and those involved weeks before you even begin. It is recommended to pray for yourself as leader, your group members, and the time you are about to spend together. It's no small thing you are about to start and the more you prepare in the Spirit, the better. Apart from Jesus, we can do nothing (John 14:5). Remain in him and "you will bear much fruit" (John 15:5). It's also a good idea to have trusted friends pray and intercede for you and your group as you work through the study.

Spiritual Battle. Like it or not, the Bible teaches that we are in the middle of a spiritual battle. The enemy would like nothing more than for this study to be ineffective. It would be part of his scheme to have group members not show up or engage in any discussion. His victory would be that your group just passes time together going through the motions of a just another Bible study. You, as a leader, are a threat to the enemy as it is your desire to lead people down the path of righteousness (as taught in Proverbs). Read Ephesians 6:10–20 and put your armor on.

Scripture. Prepare before your study by reading the selected Scripture verses ahead of time.

Chapters. Each chapter contains approximately three lessons. As you work through the lessons, keep in mind the particular chapter theme in connection with the lessons. These lessons are designed so that you can go through them in thirty minutes each.

Lessons. Each lesson has teaching points with their own discussion questions. This format should keep the participants engaged with the text and one another.

Food for Thought. The questions at the end of the teaching points are there to create discussion and deepen the connection between each person and the content being addressed. You know the people in your group and should feel free to come up with your own questions or adapt the ones provided to best meet the needs of your group. Again, this would require some preparation beforehand.

Opening and Closing Prayers. Sometimes prayer prompts are given before and usually after each lesson. These are just suggestions. You know your group and the needs present, so please feel free to pray accordingly.

Bible Commentary. The Theology of Work series contains a variety of books to help you apply the Scriptures and Christian faith to your work. This Bible study is based on the *Theology of Work Bible Commentary*, examining what the Bible says about work. This commentary is intended to assist those with theological training or interest to conduct in-depth research into passages or books of Scripture.

Video Clips. The Theology of Work website (www.theologyofwork .org) provides good video footage of people from the marketplace highlighting the teaching from all the books of the Bible. It would be great to incorporate some of these videos into your teaching time.

Enjoy your study! Remember that God's word does not return void—ever. It produces fruit and succeeds in whatever way God has intended it to succeed.

> "So shall my word be that goes out from my mouth;
> it shall not return to me empty,
> but it shall accomplish that which I purpose,
> and shall succeed in the thing for which I sent it." (Isa. 55:11)

"This commentary was written exactly for those of us who aim to integrate our faith and work on a daily basis and is an excellent reminder that God hasn't called the world to go to the church, but has called the Church to go to the world."

BONNIE WURZBACHER

FORMER SENIOR VICE PRESIDENT, THE COCA-COLA COMPANY

 THEOLOGY OF WORK   PROJECT